She
Persisted

WILMA MANKILLER

—INSPIRED BY—

She Persisted

by Chelsea Clinton & Alexandra Boiger

· ·

WILMA MANKILLER

· ·

Written by
Traci Sorell

Interior illustrations by
Gillian Flint

PHILOMEL

Philomel Books
An imprint of Penguin Random House LLC, New York

First published in the United States of America by Philomel Books,
an imprint of Penguin Random House LLC, 2022

Visit us online at penguinrandomhouse.com

Library of Congress Cataloging-in-Publication Data is available.

Printed in the United States of America

HC ISBN 9780593403037
10 9 8 7 6 5 4 3 2 1
PB ISBN 9780593403051
10 9 8 7 6 5 4 3 2 1

WOR

Edited by Jill Santopolo and Talia Benamy.
Design by Ellice M. Lee.
Text set in LTC Kennerley.

ೞ *To* ೞ
the Cherokee Nation
and Chief Mankiller's family

She Persisted

She Persisted: WANGARI MAATHAI

She Persisted: WILMA MANKILLER

She Persisted: PATSY MINK

She Persisted: SALLY RIDE

She Persisted: MARGARET CHASE SMITH

She Persisted: SONIA SOTOMAYOR

She Persisted: MARIA TALLCHIEF

She Persisted: DIANA TAURASI

She Persisted: HARRIET TUBMAN

She Persisted: OPRAH WINFREY

She Persisted: MALALA YOUSAFZAI

Dear Reader,

As Sally Ride and Marian Wright Edelman both powerfully said, "You can't be what you can't see." When Sally said that, she meant that it was hard to dream of being an astronaut, like she was, or a doctor or an athlete or anything at all if you didn't see someone like you who already had lived that dream. She especially was talking about seeing women in jobs that historically were held by men.

I wrote the first *She Persisted* and the books that came after it because I wanted young girls—and children of all genders—to see women who worked hard to live their dreams. And I wanted all of us to see examples of persistence in the face of different challenges to help inspire us in our own lives.

I'm so thrilled now to partner with a sisterhood of writers to bring longer, more in-depth versions of these stories of women's persistence and achievement to readers. I hope you enjoy these chapter books as much as I do and find them inspiring and empowering.

And remember: If anyone ever tells you no, if anyone ever says your voice isn't important or your dreams are too big, remember these women. They persisted and so should you.

Warmly,

Chelsea Clinton

WILMA MANKILLER

TABLE OF CONTENTS

....

CHAPTER 1

DⱢGꞀ·C ꞓꞀᎮ ꝺVTL
A Girl Called Pearl

Wilma Pearl Mankiller led the Cherokee Nation as its first female chief. But before she visited with US presidents and met with world leaders, she was known by family and friends as a girl called Pearl.

Pearl arrived in late autumn on November 18, 1945. Born at the old Hastings Hospital in Tahlequah, Oklahoma, she already had five siblings waiting at home for her. Her father, Charley, was a Cherokee Nation citizen living in the nearby Rocky Mountain community. Irene, her mother, was a white woman whose family had moved to the area. Her parents grew up around each other and married young. When Pearl was three, Charley built a four-room wood home for the family on land owned by his father.

Traditionally, Cherokee individuals did not own land on the tribe's reservation. The Cherokee Nation, meaning all the people in the tribe, shared the land together. Families owned their homes, gardens and crops, but not the land itself. But the US government did not want the Cherokee people to continue living together and sharing land this way. So the US Congress passed a law to divide up the tribe's reservation. Each Cherokee person received land. That is how Pearl's grandfather received the land where his family lived.

But originally, all Cherokee people lived on the tribe's lands in the Southeast, not on the reservation within what would later become northeastern Oklahoma.

In 1838, the US government rounded up Cherokee people like Pearl's ancestors at gunpoint to force them to move west. They couldn't pack up their homes or bring their animals. Over four thousand Cherokee young and old—died during the roundup before the forced march and also along the way. That means one-fourth of the tribe's population died. Lots of children became orphans. Many Native Nations also suffered similar removals from their own homelands and a horrific loss of lives.

Pearl learned some of this difficult history

while growing up on Mankiller Flats. This is what people called the land that her grandfather and others in his family had been assigned to live on.

Just like her ancestors', Pearl's life wasn't always easy while she was growing up. The tiny tin-roofed house her father built had no running water or electricity. That meant no flushing toilet, no sink with running water, and no television to watch. This was normal for homes in that area in the 1940s and 1950s.

Many Cherokee people at that time found it hard to find regular work. The rocky soil was not good for farming. Pearl's dad and oldest brother went all the way to southeastern Colorado each summer to work, harvesting crops to earn money.

Everyone had chores to do at home, from chopping wood to hauling water. Pearl and her

sisters hauled water from a cold spring a quarter
mile away to their house for cooking, cleaning
clothes and baths. Pearl worked hard to get out of

hauling water. She preferred to play in the woods instead.

The Mankiller home lacked many features that most people regularly use today. Their heat came from a wood-burning stove, which was where they made their meals too. Cutting and hauling wood for the stove was critical. Instead of electricity, they used coal-oil lamps after sunset to see each other and read books.

And Pearl and her family wore hand-me-down clothes or shirts and pants their mother made from large flour sacks. They didn't have a washing machine or a dryer, so they cleaned their clothing outside in a tub and hung it up to dry. Before winter, each child would get a coat and a pair of leather shoes.

But nothing was unique about how the

Mankiller family lived. Most of the Cherokee families around them lived just like they did. They also grew their own food as well as hunted, fished and gathered plants growing in the woods, just like their ancestors. Pearl always had enough to eat, even if her family did not have modern conveniences.

Outside of chores at home and attending school, the Mankiller family enjoyed visiting with other families at their homes and occasionally at church or at Cherokee ceremonial grounds. Often the Mankillers had guests at their house too. Many of the people spoke Cherokee, including Pearl's father.

Storytelling and visiting were a big part of Pearl's childhood. She and her siblings loved their father's stories. Her house was always full of

books, which fostered a love of reading in Pearl.

Pearl attended first through fifth grade in a small schoolhouse, full of mostly other Cherokee children. She and her siblings walked three miles each way to school no matter the weather. There was no school bus. At school, Pearl learned that others lived differently than her family. The female teachers wore lipstick and dressed more formally than most women in the Rocky Mountain community. One of the male teachers even had a television in his house!

All in all, Pearl's childhood was a happy one.

But as much as Pearl loved life in Mankiller Flats, some parts of her life were out of her—and her family's—control. The US government, which had treated her people so terribly decades earlier, would again cause turmoil and heartbreak for her family.

iLᏢ DᏪGᏋᎦ TEᎾSᎾ ᎤᎠᏖLᏁᏕᎢ

Bay Area Blues

In 1956, Congress passed a law called the Indian Relocation Act. Officials in Washington, DC, believed that Native people would be better off leaving their homes and moving to cities all over the country to work. They wanted Native people to assimilate, and they often wanted the land that had belonged to Native families for generations. Assimilation meant that Native people would have to leave their own culture, language and homelands behind and become like white people. The federal agency promised them help with job training and housing.

Many families from a variety of Native Nations chose or were forced to relocate because of poverty.

Pearl's father also wanted to have regular work to provide for his family. Pearl's mother hated the idea of leaving their home, but the idea of living closer to her mother, who had moved east of San Francisco, won her over.

As her parents and older brother discussed relocating to the San Francisco Bay Area, Pearl and her siblings grew terrified at leaving the only home they had ever known and loved. Her older sister, who attended Sequoyah High School in Tahlequah, would stay behind. With three children born after Pearl, eight Mankiller children would be moving to California.

A month before Pearl's eleventh birthday, the family loaded up in a neighbor's car for a ride to the train station. The kids looked out the windows, trying to memorize the house, the school and all the familiar scenery of home.

Many tears fell on the two-day train ride from Stilwell, Oklahoma, through Kansas City and on out to San Francisco. When they got there, they learned that their assigned apartment wouldn't be ready for another two weeks. They had to stay in an old hotel until then.

Arriving in the big city shocked everyone. The wail of loud sirens, flashing neon lights and people with no homes sleeping in doorways showed them a world they didn't know or understand. None of them had ever used a flushing toilet, turned on a light switch, or ridden in an elevator. No one came from the federal agency to offer them any welcome or answer their questions. There was so much to suddenly learn!

Gone was the familiar community, school and loved ones back home who called her by her middle name, Pearl. The girl everyone now called Wilma and her family had to figure out city life.

Their assigned apartment in a working-class neighborhood was very small and crowded. Wilma's dad went to work in a nearby rope factory; and because the family couldn't afford to live on her father's forty-eight dollars a week paycheck alone, her oldest brother worked there as well. Another baby boy soon joined the family.

Kids at school teased the Mankiller children

about their last name. Back home it was a familiar Cherokee last name. It came from the role Wilma's ancestor had as a warrior in his village back before the forced removal. But in San Francisco, the name drew all kinds of negative attention. Classmates also made fun of the Mankiller kids' accents, clothes and darker skin. She and her siblings had never ridden on bikes or used roller skates. It felt like going to school with children from another planet. Their peers had such different life experiences.

While Wilma excelled at reading, she lost interest in school. Her lack of common experiences with junior high classmates like talking on a telephone separated her from them. And even after the family saved and moved to a bigger place, Wilma felt lost in the middle of such a large family. No one seemed to understand her. She didn't understand herself or her changing body, and no one—not even her mother—explained what was happening.

Wilma ran away several times. Each time, she'd save her babysitting money and buy a bus ticket to her grandma's house over an hour away from the San Francisco Bay Area. Her parents finally saw how much she hated living in the city and let her spend a year with her grandma working on her ranch. She opened up about her struggles, adopted her grandma's work ethic and enjoyed going to school again, even making a few friends while she was there.

After eighth grade, Wilma returned from her grandma's to find that her oldest brother had gotten married and moved out. The family lost their home and moved into a low-income neighborhood where Wilma's father could support the family with just

his income. Soon another baby brother would join them.

In their new neighborhood, the Mankillers' neighbors were mostly Black, with some Samoan, Filipino, and a few Native families nearby as well. Wilma saw that it wasn't just relocated Native families who had a hard time surviving in the city—many other groups of people did too. She still struggled to connect with other classmates in school or care about her grades. Living there taught Wilma being poor in the city was more difficult than back in Mankiller Flats.

While the city may have been a hard place to live, the American Indian Center always felt like home. Housed in an old building in San Francisco's Mission District, the Center was a space for relocated Native people to gather and spend

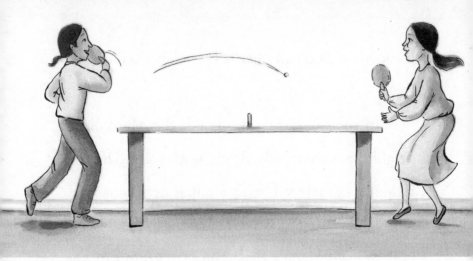

time together. Children went on outings. Teens, including Wilma, played Ping-Pong and had dance parties. Adults played bingo and talked about issues they faced in the city, including how the relocation program was a disaster for Native people.

Young people in the Bay Area, including Natives, wanted social change such as equal rights for non-white people and women, and they started to take action. Some of the Mankiller siblings did too. And Wilma was one of them.

DWSCᕼ Dᕼ OꚙWᐱVᕼ LθᕼᕼᕼᕠET

Alcatraz and Activism

The 1960s were a decade of social change. Black, Native, Chicano, and other peoples in the San Francisco Bay Area spoke out about their mistreatment in schools and communities and by police and elected officials. They wanted more access to better schools, colleges, jobs and housing that they saw white people receiving. They demanded elected officials do the right thing now.

Wilma noticed this changing world as she

graduated from high school in 1963. She soon got married and gave birth to two daughters before she turned twenty-one. While busy caring for her family, Wilma wanted to spend time helping those in the community too.

In November 1969, almost ninety Native men, women and children of all ages occupied and reclaimed the deserted island of Alcatraz in the San Francisco Bay for Native people. They wanted to help draw attention to how badly the US government treated Native Nations.

Not too long before this occupation, the US government had operated a maximum-security prison there! Because the waters of the San Francisco Bay are so cold, escaping from the prison and surviving the swim to shore was impossible. Alcatraz had been the most secure prison in the

country. But with a lack of fresh water and a rocky terrain, it became very expensive to keep open because all food, fresh water, clothing and other supplies had to be brought to the island. After the prison closed, a group of Native people saw an opportunity to speak out.

The takeover lasted for nineteen months. When Native people from across the country occupied the island, celebrities, politicians and news reporters visited them. Donations of food, clothes and money also arrived from all kinds of organizations. Troops of Girls Scouts and Boy Scouts delivered Christmas toys for the children. The takeover put a national spotlight on the mistreatment of Native Nations and their citizens—both those in cities as well as those still living on reservations.

Four of Wilma's siblings joined hundreds of

others on the island. While Wilma herself did not stay there, she did visit along with thousands of others. Children played and attended classes some of the parents developed, while other adults worked on issues to be addressed with the federal government. During one trip, Wilma's oldest daughter and other kids got locked inside a prison cell while playing when one of their friends pulled on a lever on the wall to see what it would do!

Wilma said those visits to Alcatraz "changed me forever."

She spent more time serving at the American Indian Center. The organization not only helped raise money for those on Alcatraz but also served as the command center taking and bringing messages back and forth between the activists and the federal government.

During this same time, her father, Charley, became ill from a kidney disease. Wilma also learned that she had inherited the same disease as her father. The entire family was stunned. When Wilma's father died, it was a difficult loss for everyone. The family took his body back to the cemetery near Mankiller Flats for burial.

A few months after the family returned from the funeral in Oklahoma, the Alcatraz occupation ended. In one of Wilma's final conversations with her father in the hospital before his death, he had told her how proud he was of her work to help those on Alcatraz and bring more awareness to the needs of relocated Indians. That talk spurred Wilma to want to do even more.

From watching the news in San Francisco, Wilma learned that there was a group of lawyers working on behalf of the nearby Pit River Tribe to reclaim their ancestral lands from a powerful electric company, and she volunteered to help, including writing grant proposals for them. While the US government admitted the tribe never ceded its lands, the Pit River Tribe wasn't successful. This experience taught Wilma about the challenges Native Nations face in exercising their sovereignty, which is their power to make laws and take care of their land and people.

Wilma also directed the Native American Youth Center in Oakland. She created many programs for young people like those she and her siblings had enjoyed at the American Indian Center across the bay in San Francisco. After school, Native kids completed their homework and got help with reading and math at the center. They also went on field trips and visits all over Northern California. Wilma recruited Native adults to help. Even though none of them had much money, everyone came together for their children.

When Wilma wasn't working, she enjoyed playing guitar and singing to her daughters, creating skits for them to act out, and writing poetry.

She even took a few college classes that interested her. This decision eased her back into a school environment. And she enjoyed it!

Wilma also became close friends with other Native woman activists. These women wanted better lives for their children and communities just like Wilma did.

All of this work, learning and service led to trouble in Wilma's marriage. Her husband wanted a wife who stayed home, focused mainly on his needs and those of their children.

But Wilma saw herself having many roles in her life. So Wilma and her husband got divorced, and though it was difficult for her and her children, Wilma knew it was the right move for her, for her daughters and for the work she wanted to do. She was ready for the next chapter in her life.

CHAPTER 4

ᎠᏏᎩᎤᎵ ᎦᏙ ᏗᎭᎤᏍᏬᎵᎦ ᎠᏓᎦᏍᏬᎡᏔ

Home to Mankiller Flats

After Wilma and her husband divorced, she found living in an expensive place like the Bay Area tough as a single mother. She had room-mates to help share costs. But she knew she needed to get home to Mankiller Flats.

Wilma's mother, Irene, had moved back to the area just a few months before Wilma, now thirty-one years old, and her daughters, now ages thirteen and eleven, packed up the moving truck and headed east in the summer of 1977. The three of them stayed with Irene while Wilma looked for work. When not applying for jobs, Wilma sewed clothes and played her guitar to keep her spirits up.

Finally, fall arrived, and Wilma got hired by the Cherokee Nation. Once the tribe learned she had experience writing grant proposals, which were letters that helped get money for important projects, that soon became the focus of her job. She also took classes to finish her own college degree in social work and enrolled in graduate school.

Then tragedy struck.

One day, as Wilma headed to the Cherokee Nation's offices in Tahlequah, a small car hit her old station wagon head-on as it tried to pass two other slower cars while heading up a hill. Wilma suffered a lot of injuries—two broken legs, many broken ribs, and a crushed face.

Thankfully, ambulances arrived quickly and got her to the hospital. Eventually she'd have seventeen surgeries to recover from the crash, wearing casts on both legs for a while. What Wilma lost forever though that day was her very good friend Sherry Morris—the driver of the other car. They loved spending time together and had plans before the accident happened to go shopping that upcoming weekend for an oak table that Sherry wanted.

During her time at home recovering, Wilma mourned the loss of her dear friend and reflected on how she had faced death and survived. She focused on "being of good mind" as Cherokee elders teach, using this experience as something to move forward from in a positive way. The care from her family and their help with her daughters helped Wilma stay focused on walking again by herself.

But her troubles were not over. Just a couple of months after her accident, Wilma experienced muscle problems. Holding a pencil, brushing her teeth, or combing her hair proved impossible, as she couldn't maintain a grip on anything. Then she suffered severe double vision.

Doctors could not figure out what happened to cause this loss of strength. Not until several months later, as Wilma watched a live TV show raising money for muscular diseases, did she learn what she had. When a woman with a disease called myasthenia gravis explained her muscle problems, Wilma realized she shared identical symptoms!

Wilma's sister took her to a doctor for testing. The results confirmed that she had the same disease as the woman on TV, which can lead to paralysis. Once again, Wilma required surgery—followed by strong medicine to help her body recover. She continued to focus on being of good mind and doing everything required to heal.

Over a year after the car accident, Wilma returned to work for the Cherokee Nation. She again crafted and submitted grant proposals for the tribe. She also wrote her first fictional short story during this time to help her process what she'd endured. It got published a few years later.

Not long after she began working full-time

again, Wilma was chosen to run the Cherokee Nation Community Development Department, which was responsible for securing money to help communities across the reservation survive and thrive. She focused on finding funding for projects to help Cherokee people address their needs—like those in the rural community of Bell, which wasn't far from Mankiller Flats.

Nearly everyone in Bell was Cherokee, and most of them spoke the Cherokee language. The community needed indoor plumbing for kitchens, bathrooms and laundry rooms in every home, so residents could stop hauling water to use for everything.

Wilma relied on Charlie Soap, a Cherokee co-worker who spoke both English and Cherokee, to explain the some details to Bell residents. As her co-organizer, he described in Cherokee that while

the tribe would help raise funds from the US
government for the materials like the sixteen miles
of pipe they needed, community members would
have to fill out paperwork about themselves,

volunteer their labor to dig the trenches, and help
lay and connect the pipe. Almost no one had experience doing this. But once the materials arrived,
everyone got to work!

After the community completed the project,

a major TV network came to film their success. Wilma said that the Bell project affirmed for her how Cherokee people have a "willingness to pitch in and help one another."

But Wilma's ability to bring Cherokee people together and address their own challenges didn't stop there.

CHAPTER 5

SᎦᎣꞋRT ᏚᏉᏢ ᎠᏏᏴᎾ

Leading Her People

Wilma's success with the Bell waterline project and grant writing caught the attention of the Cherokee Nation's principal chief. He invited her to run as his deputy chief in the upcoming 1983 election.

Having just overcome his own health challenges, Chief Swimmer appreciated Wilma's dedication to her work and to helping Cherokee citizens. But many in his campaign did not share his views. And they weren't the only ones.

Wilma found many Cherokee men and women believed she was not qualified for the position. True, she'd never held an elected position before. But her years of grassroots organizing, volunteering to help the Pit River Tribe with their treaty rights, and strong work ethic made her a powerful candidate.

Through all of this, Chief Swimmer never wavered in his support. More importantly, Wilma stayed strong and outspoken—even when some people threatened her life. She dedicated herself to the campaign, and even quit her job with the Cherokee Nation and used her own savings to pay for campaign expenses.

In the end, the people Wilma had worked with in various communities showed up to vote, and other Cherokees joined them to elect her as the deputy chief. She won!

In her new role, Deputy Chief Mankiller served as the president of the tribal council. She also helped oversee the tribe's more than forty programs. She was busy.

In fall of 1985, US President Ronald Reagan changed everything for the Cherokee Nation. He invited Chief Swimmer to join him in Washington, DC, and serve as his Assistant Secretary of the Interior for Indian Affairs. Swimmer accepted.

With Swimmer gone from his role as principal chief, Wilma was next in line. She took the oath as required by the tribe's constitution to step in and serve as principal chief. Media professionals, family, community members and guests packed the council chamber as Wilma was sworn

in. After the applause stopped, now Principal Chief Mankiller, the tribe's first female head of government, walked to the podium and thanked everyone.

Then she got back to work.

Her family worried, though, that the now forty-year-old leader's health would suffer with her schedule becoming even busier than before.

Thankfully, Chief Mankiller had a solid support network around her. The next fall, she married one of her biggest supporters—her friend and former colleague Charlie Soap. Charlie adored Wilma's leadership and strength and had never been intimidated by it. They loved each other very much.

Their partnership saw Wilma through more health challenges during her 1987 campaign for

principal chief. In the final weeks before the election, her kidney problems resurfaced. Her team of supporters visited with Cherokee families for her while Charlie focused on visiting with those fluent Cherokee speakers living in rural areas.

Despite her hospitalizations, Wilma beat her opponent and became the first elected female principal chief of the Cherokee Nation. Now she could continue the work she'd started to strengthen the tribe's economy and make sure they had the money they needed.

Wilma was different from the men who had served as chief of the Cherokee Nation before her. They had not grown up in poverty like she had. That experience helped many people vote for her because they felt she knew the hardships they faced and would work to address them. And that's exactly what she did.

Because Chief Mankiller had watched her own family struggle to earn enough money, her administration focused on developing businesses in rural areas to provide steady, year-round employment for Cherokee people. The foundation of Cherokee Nation's gaming and hospitality businesses started under her leadership. She also saved a job training program for young people on the Cherokee reservation from closing. And her administration opened more health clinics and supported funding for education so that members of the Cherokee Nation could have access to healthcare and schools.

Cherokee people noticed her efforts and reelected her in 1991 with an overwhelming majority of the vote. They wanted Wilma! Just before her reelection, though, Chief Mankiller's health problems cropped up again. This time, polycystic kidney disease had caused her kidneys to fail. Luckily, her older brother was able to donate one of his kidneys to her, and she survived.

Chief Mankiller recovered from the kidney surgery, and she kept on working. She signed a self-governance agreement with the federal government, which was a contract that allowed the Cherokee Nation to decide how to spend their federal funding, rather than leaving it in the hands of a federal agency.

Even as she faced health challenges, Wilma kept her focus on making sure that the Cherokee Nation was in control of its own future and was giving its tribal citizens what they needed. But when she was diagnosed with lymphoma, a type of cancer, in 1995, she decided not to run again. Her time as principal chief would be over. But that didn't mean the world would stop feeling her presence.

ᏍᏏ ᎣᏅᏂᏗ ᎥᎬᎡ ᎠᎯᏛᎢ

Inspiring Others

After Wilma Mankiller recovered from her cancer, she kept on encouraging, mentoring and inspiring others. She found more time to write, sharing her thoughts in books. She noted that most of the information out there about Cherokee people hadn't been written by Cherokee people. Seeing this, she observed that "the voices of our grandmothers are silenced by most of the written history of our people." She knew she could help change that.

Wilma wrote about the major roles women had always played in the Cherokee Nation and other tribal societies. In her writings and talks, she made sure to include their contributions and accomplishments—both past and present.

Beyond her written and spoken teachings, Wilma had a great impact.

In 1998, US President Bill Clinton awarded

her the Presidential Medal of Freedom. This is the highest honor in the United States for civilians— people who are not in the military or police force. Those receiving the award have made outstanding contributions to national security, world peace, culture or other important areas. Wilma's achievements deserved such recognition.

Even as she continued her work, Wilma's health got worse again. Later in the same year that she received the Medal of Freedom, Wilma required a second kidney transplant. The radiation treatments from cancer had damaged the kidney her brother had donated. This time one of her nieces donated a kidney, allowing Wilma to continue helping and inspiring others.

Beyond her work and taking care of her health, Wilma also enjoyed spending more time with her family. "Grandma Chief," as some of her grandkids and their friends called her, cheered loudly when attending their activities and sporting events.

In a speech less than two years before her death, Chief Mankiller shared that "dreams can never be colonized." That means nobody can control what one sees or wishes for their own future. Certainly her statement rings true for her own life as well. While the young girl they called Pearl never dreamed of leading the Cherokee Nation, her service to the tribe as its chief has given the world a wonderful example of what female leaders can accomplish and what leaders can look like.

Wilma Pearl Mankiller died on April 6, 2010, from pancreatic cancer. Upon hearing of her death, Indigenous leaders across the planet lit fires to help Wilma on her journey home to become an ancestor. Her life provides a courageous example of persistence and service to others despite numerous hardships—for each and every one of us.

HOW YOU CAN PERSIST

by Traci Sorell

Chief Wilma Mankiller faced many obstacles in her life, but she persisted in keeping a positive outlook and using her gifts to help and lead others. If you would like to honor Chief Mankiller's legacy, here are some things you can do:

1. Whether you are a citizen of a Native Nation or not, learn more about Native Nations across this continent and

how they live today. Start with those closest to you at native-land.ca or begin with the Cherokee Nation. Read more about the tribe and its citizens today at visitcherokeenation.com and watch its TV series osiyo.tv.

2. Visit with your family and elders. Listen to their stories. Create stories of your own to share.

3. Welcome new students to your school. Learn their names and say them correctly. Accept how they talk, dress or move in the world as part of who they are.

4. Find out who might need assistance within your community. Volunteer your time and ask others to help too.

5. Express yourself through art—sing, play an instrument, write, dance, act, draw or paint.

6. Remember that we each have different paths to walk in life. Stay true to yours and let others have theirs.

7. Practice gadugi (gah-doo-ghee/ᏍᏉᎩ), the Cherokee value of working together, and combine your talents with others to serve everyone.

ACKNOWLEDGMENTS

For Chief Wilma Mankiller tsigesv (jee-gay-suh/ᏥᎦᏴ), who helped others regardless of her own hardships or what others around her thought, said or did.

For Wilma's daughters, Gina and Felicia Olaya, for sharing some childhood memories.

For Charlie Soap and Kristina Kiehl, who provided reference photos for the interior art.

For John Ross, who provided the Cherokee syllabary for each chapter title.

For the staff at the Western History Archives at the University of Oklahoma, who helped me access Chief Mankiller's donated files—all of which served as critical sources.

For the Tulsa Artist Fellowship funding, which supported my time to write this book.

For my mother, Carolyn J. McClellan, who has always believed in me and encouraged me in every endeavor I pursue—including creating works for young people.

For young people facing difficulties, keep persisting and use your gifts for the greater good.

ABOUT THE COVER

The seven-pointed star on the book's cover represents the seven clans or groups within the Cherokee Nation. Traditionally, a child receives their clan from their mother. Each clan has certain responsibilities in their community and ceremonial life. The seven-pointed star appears on the Cherokee Nation governmental seal and its flag.

NOTE ON TERMS

"Indian," "American Indian," "Native American," "Native" and "Indigenous" are all used to describe the peoples who originally lived on this land and continue to do so, even since the formation of the United States.

The label "Indian" came from Christopher Columbus. He wrongly believed he had landed on the Indian subcontinent, instead of encountering Taíno people on the Caribbean island that the countries of the Dominican Republic and Haiti now share. As a result of his error, "Indian" becomes the word found in the Declaration of Independence, the United States Constitution, other federal laws and the names of federal agencies like the Indian Health Service and the Bureau of Indian Affairs. This was the word used when Wilma Mankiller was growing up.

Sometimes "American" is added before "Indian" or the term "Native American" is used, but these are incorrect too. Native Nations and their citizens lived on this big continent long before it was given the name "America." This happened because Italian navigator Amerigo Vespucci sailed around the large land mass and realized it was a separate continent and not part of Asia.

More recently, "Native people," "Natives," "Indigenous" and "Indigenous peoples" are words used to describe the original people of this land. But it's important to remember that all those people come from a variety of Nations and have specific names that they call themselves, which is the best way to refer to them. For example, Wilma Mankiller and other citizens of her same tribe refer to themselves as "Cherokee" because they are recognized as belonging to the Cherokee Nation.

ᴄᴐ References ᴐ

"Cherokees to Get Control of US Funds." *Los Angeles Times*. July 5, 1990. latimes.com /archives/la-xpm-1990-07-05-mn-168-story.html.

"Mankiller Gets Kidney Transplant." *The Oklahoman*. June 21, 1990. oklahoman.com /article/2321475/mankiller-gets-kidney-transplant.

Mankiller, Wilma. "Challenges Facing 21st Century Indigenous People." Simon Ortiz and Labriola Center Lecture on Indigenous Land, Culture, and Community. Arizona State University, October 2, 2008. Video, 50:42. youtube.com/watch?v=9K_rVUmV7Y8.

Mankiller, Wilma. "A Modern Pioneer in Cherokee Nation (Wilma Mankiller)." Interview by Marcia Alvar. UW Video, March 6, 2014. Video, 28:24. youtube.com/watch?v=zqqkKrz5U5Y.

Mankiller, Wilma. Transcripts of interviews by Michael Wallis. Wilma Mankiller Collection, Box 43. Western History Archives, University of Oklahoma, 1991–92.

Mankiller, Wilma, and Michael Wallis. *Mankiller: A Chief and Her People: An Autobiography of the Principal Chief of the Cherokee Nation.* New York: St. Martin's Press, 1993.

Olaya, Felicia. Correspondence with Traci Sorell. December 15, 2021.

Olaya, Gina. Interview by Traci Sorell. Tahlequah, Oklahoma. July 1, 2018.

Olaya, Gina, and Kellen Quinton. "A Mother and Son Remember 'Grandma Chief,'" *Story*

Corps, September 27, 2021. Podcast, 2:52. storycorps.org/stories/a-mother-and-son -remember-grandma-chief.

"Prison Closure." Historical Information. Federal Bureau of Prisons. bop.gov/about/history /alcatraz.jsp.

Red-Horse, Valerie, dir. *Mankiller: Activist. Feminist. Cherokee Chief.* Red Horse Native Productions, Inc, Valhalla Entertainment and Vision Maker Media, 2017.

"Wilma Mankiller: Principal Chief of the Cherokee Nation, 1985–1995." *Voices of Oklahoma.* August 13, 2009. voicesofoklahoma .com/interview/mankiller-wilma.

"Wilma Pearl Mankiller." *Muskogee Phoenix.* April 10, 2010. obituaries.muskogeephoenix .com/obituary/wilma-mankiller-748631472.

TRACI SORELL is a 2021–2022 Tulsa Artist Fellow and the award-winning author of *We Are Grateful: Otsaliheliga*, which is a Sibert, Orbis Pictus, *Boston Globe-Horn Book* and American Indian Youth Literature Award (AIYLA) Honor Book; *At the Mountain's Base* (AIYLA Honor Book); and co-author of *Indian No More*, which won the AIYLA middle grade category. Her 2021 nonfiction, middle grade works include *Classified: The Secret Career of Mary Golda Ross, Cherokee Aerospace Engineer*, an AIYLA and Orbis Pictus Honor Book, and *We Are Still Here! Native American Truths Everyone Should Know*, a Sibert and AIYLA Honor Book. A former federal Indigenous law attorney and policy advocate, Traci is an enrolled citizen of the Cherokee Nation and lives with her family on her tribe's reservation in northeastern Oklahoma.

Photo credit: Kelly Downs Photography

You can visit Traci online at
tracisorell.com
and follow her on Twitter and Instagram
@tracisorell

GILLIAN FLINT has worked as a professional illustrator since earning an animation and illustration degree in 2003. Her work has since been published in the UK, USA and Australia. In her spare time, Gillian enjoys reading, spending time with her family and puttering about in the garden on sunny days. She lives in the northwest of England.

You can visit Gillian Flint online at
gillianflint.com
or follow her on Twitter
@GillianFlint
and on Instagram
@gillianflint_illustration

CHELSEA CLINTON is the author of the #1 *New York Times* bestseller *She Persisted: 13 American Women Who Changed the World*; *She Persisted Around the World: 13 Women Who Changed History*; *She Persisted in Sports: American Olympians Who Changed the Game*; *Don't Let Them Disappear: 12 Endangered Species Across the Globe*; *It's Your World: Get Informed, Get Inspired & Get Going!*; *Start Now!: You Can Make a Difference*; with Hillary Clinton, *Grandma's Gardens* and *Gutsy Women*; and, with Devi Sridhar, *Governing Global Health: Who Runs the World and Why?* She is also the Vice Chair of the Clinton Foundation, where she works on many initiatives, including those that help empower the next generation of leaders. She lives in New York City with her husband, Marc, their children and their dog, Soren.

Courtesy of the author

You can follow Chelsea Clinton on Twitter
@ChelseaClinton
or on Facebook at
facebook.com/chelseaclinton

ALEXANDRA BOIGER has illustrated nearly twenty picture books, including the She Persisted books by Chelsea Clinton; the popular Tallulah series by Marilyn Singer; and the Max and Marla books, which she also wrote. Originally from Munich, Germany, she now lives outside of San Francisco, California, with her husband, Andrea, daughter, Vanessa, and two cats, Luiso and Winter.

You can visit Alexandra Boiger online at
alexandraboiger.com
or follow her on Instagram
@alexandra_boiger

Read about more inspiring women in the

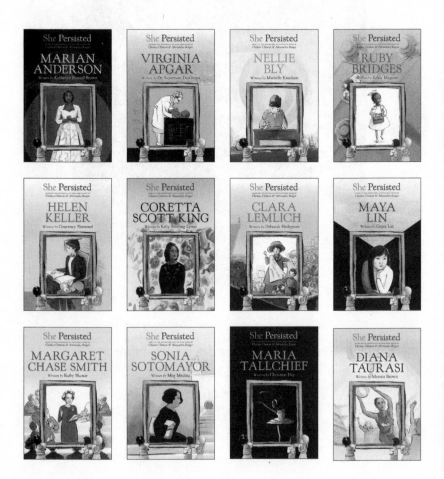